" You must go on adventures to find out where you truly belong"

~ Sue Fitzmaurie

This Book Belongs To:

Nathan & Jessica

December 2020

Let the adventures begin !!

Love,
Shelley

Bucket List Goal:

#1 _____

Inspiration for this Goal? _____

_____

_____

Steps to make this happen?_____

_____

_____

Date Completed:_____

Location:_____

Adventure Highlights and Favorite Memories:_____

_____

_____

_____

_____

_____

_____

Lessons Learned:_____

_____

_____

_____

_____

Bucket List Goal:

#2 _____

Inspiration for this Goal? _____

_____

_____

Steps to make this happen?_____

_____

_____

Date Completed:_____

Location:_____

Adventure Highlights and Favorite Memories:_____

_____

_____

_____

_____

_____

_____

Lessons Learned:_____

_____

_____

_____

_____

Bucket List Goal:

#3 _____

Inspiration for this Goal? _____

_____

_____

Steps to make this happen?_____

_____

_____

Date Completed:_____

Location:_____

Adventure Highlights and Favorite Memories:_____

_____

_____

_____

_____

_____

_____

Lessons Learned:_____

_____

_____

_____

Bucket List Goal:

#4 _____

Inspiration for this Goal? _____

_____

_____

Steps to make this happen?_____

_____

_____

Date Completed:_____

Location:_____

Adventure Highlights and Favorite Memories:_____

_____

_____

_____

_____

_____

_____

Lessons Learned:_____

_____

_____

_____

_____

Bucket List Goal:

#5 _____

Inspiration for this Goal? _____

_____

_____

Steps to make this happen?_____

_____

_____

Date Completed:_____

Location:_____

Adventure Highlights and Favorite Memories:_____

_____

_____

_____

_____

_____

_____

Lessons Learned:_____

_____

_____

_____

Bucket List Goal:

#6 _____

Inspiration for this Goal? _____

_____

_____

Steps to make this happen?_____

_____

_____

Date Completed:_____

Location:_____

Adventure Highlights and Favorite Memories:_____

_____

_____

_____

_____

_____

_____

Lessons Learned:_____

_____

_____

_____

_____

Bucket List Goal:

#7 _____

Inspiration for this Goal? _____

_____

_____

Steps to make this happen?_____

_____

_____

Date Completed:_____

Location:_____

Adventure Highlights and Favorite Memories:_____

_____

_____

_____

_____

_____

_____

Lessons Learned:_____

_____

_____

_____

_____

Bucket List Goal:

#8 _____

Inspiration for this Goal? _____

_____

_____

Steps to make this happen?_____

_____

_____

Date Completed:_____

Location:_____

Adventure Highlights and Favorite Memories:_____

_____

_____

_____

_____

_____

_____

Lessons Learned:_____

_____

_____

_____

_____

Bucket List Goal:

#9 _____

Inspiration for this Goal? _____

_____

_____

Steps to make this happen?_____

_____

_____

Date Completed:_____

Location:_____

Adventure Highlights and Favorite Memories:_____

_____

_____

_____

_____

_____

_____

Lessons Learned:_____

_____

_____

_____

_____

Bucket List Goal:
#10 _____

Inspiration for this Goal? _____
_____
_____

Steps to make this happen?_____
_____
_____

Date Completed:_____

Location:_____

Adventure Highlights and Favorite Memories:_____
_____
_____
_____
_____
_____
_____

Lessons Learned:_____
_____
_____
_____
_____

Bucket List Goal:

#11 _____

Inspiration for this Goal? _____

_____

_____

Steps to make this happen?_____

_____

_____

Date Completed:_____

Location:_____

Adventure Highlights and Favorite Memories:_____

_____

_____

_____

_____

_____

_____

Lessons Learned:_____

_____

_____

_____

Bucket List Goal:

#12 _____

Inspiration for this Goal? _____

_____

_____

Steps to make this happen?_____

_____

_____

Date Completed:_____

Location:_____

Adventure Highlights and Favorite Memories:_____

_____

_____

_____

_____

_____

_____

Lessons Learned:_____

_____

_____

_____

_____

Bucket List Goal:
#13 _____

Inspiration for this Goal? _____

_____

_____

Steps to make this happen?_____

_____

_____

Date Completed:_____

Location:_____

Adventure Highlights and Favorite Memories:_____

_____

_____

_____

_____

_____

_____

Lessons Learned:_____

_____

_____

_____

Bucket List Goal:

#14 _____

Inspiration for this Goal? _____

_____

_____

Steps to make this happen?_____

_____

_____

Date Completed:_____

Location:_____

Adventure Highlights and Favorite Memories:_____

_____

_____

_____

_____

_____

_____

Lessons Learned:_____

_____

_____

_____

Bucket List Goal:

#15 _____

Inspiration for this Goal? _____

_____

_____

Steps to make this happen?_____

_____

_____

Date Completed:_____

Location:_____

Adventure Highlights and Favorite Memories:_____

_____

_____

_____

_____

_____

_____

Lessons Learned:_____

_____

_____

_____

_____

Bucket List Goal:
#16 _____

Inspiration for this Goal? _____
_____
_____

Steps to make this happen?_____
_____
_____

Date Completed:_____

Location:_____

Adventure Highlights and Favorite Memories:_____
_____
_____
_____
_____
_____
_____

Lessons Learned:_____
_____
_____
_____

Bucket List Goal:
#17 _____

Inspiration for this Goal? _____

_____

_____

Steps to make this happen?_____

_____

_____

Date Completed:_____

Location:_____

Adventure Highlights and Favorite Memories:_____

_____

_____

_____

_____

_____

_____

Lessons Learned:_____

_____

_____

_____

_____

Bucket List Goal:

#18 _____

Inspiration for this Goal? _____

_____

_____

Steps to make this happen?_____

_____

_____

Date Completed:_____

Location:_____

Adventure Highlights and Favorite Memories:_____

_____

_____

_____

_____

_____

_____

Lessons Learned:_____

_____

_____

_____

_____

Bucket List Goal:

#19 _____

Inspiration for this Goal? _____

_____

_____

Steps to make this happen?_____

_____

_____

Date Completed:_____

Location:_____

Adventure Highlights and Favorite Memories:_____

_____

_____

_____

_____

_____

_____

Lessons Learned:_____

_____

_____

_____

_____

Bucket List Goal:

#20 _____

Inspiration for this Goal? _____

_____

_____

Steps to make this happen?_____

_____

_____

Date Completed:_____

Location:_____

Adventure Highlights and Favorite Memories:_____

_____

_____

_____

_____

_____

_____

Lessons Learned:_____

_____

_____

_____

_____

Bucket List Goal:

#21 _____

Inspiration for this Goal? _____

_____

_____

Steps to make this happen?_____

_____

_____

Date Completed:_____

Location:_____

Adventure Highlights and Favorite Memories:_____

_____

_____

_____

_____

_____

_____

Lessons Learned:_____

_____

_____

_____

Bucket List Goal:

#22 _____

Inspiration for this Goal? _____

_____

_____

Steps to make this happen?_____

_____

_____

Date Completed:_____

Location:_____

Adventure Highlights and Favorite Memories:_____

_____

_____

_____

_____

_____

_____

Lessons Learned:_____

_____

_____

_____

_____

Bucket List Goal:

#23 _____

Inspiration for this Goal? _____

_____

_____

Steps to make this happen?_____

_____

_____

Date Completed:_____

Location:_____

Adventure Highlights and Favorite Memories:_____

_____

_____

_____

_____

_____

_____

Lessons Learned:_____

_____

_____

_____

_____

Bucket List Goal:

#24 _____

Inspiration for this Goal? _____

_____

_____

Steps to make this happen?_____

_____

_____

Date Completed:_____

Location:_____

Adventure Highlights and Favorite Memories:_____

_____

_____

_____

_____

_____

_____

Lessons Learned:_____

_____

_____

_____

_____

Bucket List Goal:

#25 _____

Inspiration for this Goal? _____

_____

_____

Steps to make this happen?_____

_____

_____

Date Completed:_____

Location:_____

Adventure Highlights and Favorite Memories:_____

_____

_____

_____

_____

_____

_____

Lessons Learned:_____

_____

_____

_____

_____

Bucket List Goal:
#26 _____

Inspiration for this Goal? _____
_____
_____

Steps to make this happen?_____
_____
_____

Date Completed:_____

Location:_____

Adventure Highlights and Favorite Memories:_____
_____
_____
_____
_____
_____
_____

Lessons Learned:_____
_____
_____
_____
_____

Bucket List Goal:
#27 _____

Inspiration for this Goal? _____

_____

_____

Steps to make this happen?_____

_____

_____

Date Completed:_____

Location:_____

Adventure Highlights and Favorite Memories:_____

_____

_____

_____

_____

_____

_____

Lessons Learned:_____

_____

_____

_____

_____

Bucket List Goal:

#28 _____

Inspiration for this Goal? _____

_____

_____

Steps to make this happen?_____

_____

_____

Date Completed:_____

Location:_____

Adventure Highlights and Favorite Memories:_____

_____

_____

_____

_____

_____

_____

Lessons Learned:_____

_____

_____

_____

Bucket List Goal:

#29 _____

Inspiration for this Goal? _____

_____

_____

Steps to make this happen?_____

_____

_____

Date Completed:_____

Location:_____

Adventure Highlights and Favorite Memories:_____

_____

_____

_____

_____

_____

_____

Lessons Learned:_____

_____

_____

_____

_____

Bucket List Goal:
#30 _____

Inspiration for this Goal? _____
_____
_____

Steps to make this happen?_____
_____
_____

Date Completed:_____

Location:_____

Adventure Highlights and Favorite Memories:_____
_____
_____
_____
_____
_____
_____

Lessons Learned:_____
_____
_____
_____
_____

Bucket List Goal:
#31 _____

Inspiration for this Goal? _____

_____

_____

Steps to make this happen?_____

_____

_____

Date Completed:_____

Location:_____

Adventure Highlights and Favorite Memories:_____

_____

_____

_____

_____

_____

_____

Lessons Learned:_____

_____

_____

_____

Bucket List Goal:

#32 _____

Inspiration for this Goal? _____
_____
_____

Steps to make this happen?_____
_____
_____

Date Completed:_____

Location:_____

Adventure Highlights and Favorite Memories:_____
_____
_____
_____
_____
_____
_____

Lessons Learned:_____
_____
_____
_____
_____

Bucket List Goal:

#33 _____

Inspiration for this Goal? _____

_____

_____

Steps to make this happen?_____

_____

_____

Date Completed:_____

Location:_____

Adventure Highlights and Favorite Memories:_____

_____

_____

_____

_____

_____

_____

Lessons Learned:_____

_____

_____

_____

_____

Bucket List Goal:

#34 _____

Inspiration for this Goal? _____

_____

_____

Steps to make this happen?_____

_____

_____

Date Completed:_____

Location:_____

Adventure Highlights and Favorite Memories:_____

_____

_____

_____

_____

_____

_____

Lessons Learned:_____

_____

_____

_____

_____

Bucket List Goal:

#35 _____

Inspiration for this Goal? _____

_____

_____

Steps to make this happen?_____

_____

_____

Date Completed:_____

Location:_____

Adventure Highlights and Favorite Memories:_____

_____

_____

_____

_____

_____

_____

Lessons Learned:_____

_____

_____

_____

_____

Bucket List Goal:

#36 _____

Inspiration for this Goal? _____

_____

_____

Steps to make this happen?_____

_____

_____

Date Completed:_____

Location:_____

Adventure Highlights and Favorite Memories:_____

_____

_____

_____

_____

_____

_____

Lessons Learned:_____

_____

_____

_____

_____

Bucket List Goal:
#37 _____

Inspiration for this Goal? _____

_____

_____

Steps to make this happen?_____

_____

_____

Date Completed:_____

Location:_____

Adventure Highlights and Favorite Memories:_____

_____

_____

_____

_____

_____

_____

Lessons Learned:_____

_____

_____

_____

_____

Bucket List Goal:

#38 _____

Inspiration for this Goal? _____

_____

_____

Steps to make this happen?_____

_____

_____

Date Completed:_____

Location:_____

Adventure Highlights and Favorite Memories:_____

_____

_____

_____

_____

_____

_____

Lessons Learned:_____

_____

_____

_____

_____

Bucket List Goal:

#39 _____

Inspiration for this Goal? _____

_____

_____

Steps to make this happen?_____

_____

_____

Date Completed:_____

Location:_____

Adventure Highlights and Favorite Memories:_____

_____

_____

_____

_____

_____

_____

Lessons Learned:_____

_____

_____

_____

_____

Bucket List Goal:

#40 _____

Inspiration for this Goal? _____

_____

_____

Steps to make this happen?_____

_____

_____

Date Completed:_____

Location:_____

Adventure Highlights and Favorite Memories:_____

_____

_____

_____

_____

_____

_____

Lessons Learned:_____

_____

_____

_____

_____

Bucket List Goal:
#41 _____

Inspiration for this Goal? _____

_____

_____

Steps to make this happen?_____

_____

_____

Date Completed:_____

Location:_____

Adventure Highlights and Favorite Memories:_____

_____

_____

_____

_____

_____

_____

Lessons Learned:_____

_____

_____

_____

_____

Bucket List Goal:

#42 _____

Inspiration for this Goal? _____

_____

_____

Steps to make this happen?_____

_____

_____

Date Completed:_____

Location:_____

Adventure Highlights and Favorite Memories:_____

_____

_____

_____

_____

_____

_____

Lessons Learned:_____

_____

_____

_____

_____

Bucket List Goal:

#43 _____

Inspiration for this Goal? _____

_____

_____

Steps to make this happen?_____

_____

_____

Date Completed:_____

Location:_____

Adventure Highlights and Favorite Memories:_____

_____

_____

_____

_____

_____

_____

Lessons Learned:_____

_____

_____

_____

_____

Bucket List Goal:

#44 _____

Inspiration for this Goal? _____
_____
_____

Steps to make this happen?_____
_____
_____

Date Completed:_____

Location:_____

Adventure Highlights and Favorite Memories:_____
_____
_____
_____
_____
_____
_____

Lessons Learned:_____
_____
_____
_____

Bucket List Goal:

#45 _____

Inspiration for this Goal? _____

_____

_____

Steps to make this happen?_____

_____

_____

Date Completed:_____

Location:_____

Adventure Highlights and Favorite Memories:_____

_____

_____

_____

_____

_____

_____

Lessons Learned:_____

_____

_____

_____

Bucket List Goal:

#46 _____

Inspiration for this Goal? _____

_____

_____

Steps to make this happen?_____

_____

_____

Date Completed:_____

Location:_____

Adventure Highlights and Favorite Memories:_____

_____

_____

_____

_____

_____

_____

Lessons Learned:_____

_____

_____

_____

_____

Bucket List Goal:
#47 _____

Inspiration for this Goal? _____

_____

_____

Steps to make this happen?_____

_____

_____

Date Completed:_____

Location:_____

Adventure Highlights and Favorite Memories:_____

_____

_____

_____

_____

_____

_____

Lessons Learned:_____

_____

_____

_____

_____

Bucket List Goal:

#48 _____

Inspiration for this Goal? _____

_____

_____

Steps to make this happen?_____

_____

_____

Date Completed:_____

Location:_____

Adventure Highlights and Favorite Memories:_____

_____

_____

_____

_____

_____

_____

Lessons Learned:_____

_____

_____

_____

Bucket List Goal:

#49 _____

Inspiration for this Goal? _____

_____

_____

Steps to make this happen?_____

_____

_____

Date Completed:_____

Location:_____

Adventure Highlights and Favorite Memories:_____

_____

_____

_____

_____

_____

_____

Lessons Learned:_____

_____

_____

_____

Bucket List Goal:

#50 _____

Inspiration for this Goal? _____

_____

_____

Steps to make this happen?_____

_____

_____

Date Completed:_____

Location:_____

Adventure Highlights and Favorite Memories:_____

_____

_____

_____

_____

_____

Lessons Learned:_____

_____

_____

_____

Bucket List Goal:

#51 _____

Inspiration for this Goal? _____

_____

_____

Steps to make this happen?_____

_____

_____

Date Completed:_____

Location:_____

Adventure Highlights and Favorite Memories:_____

_____

_____

_____

_____

_____

_____

Lessons Learned:_____

_____

_____

_____

_____

Bucket List Goal:

#52 _____

Inspiration for this Goal? _____

_____

_____

Steps to make this happen?_____

_____

_____

Date Completed:_____

Location:_____

Adventure Highlights and Favorite Memories:_____

_____

_____

_____

_____

_____

_____

Lessons Learned:_____

_____

_____

_____

Bucket List Goal:

#53 _____

Inspiration for this Goal? _____

_____

_____

Steps to make this happen?_____

_____

_____

Date Completed:_____

Location:_____

Adventure Highlights and Favorite Memories:_____

_____

_____

_____

_____

_____

_____

Lessons Learned:_____

_____

_____

_____

Bucket List Goal:

#54 _____

Inspiration for this Goal? _____

_____

_____

Steps to make this happen?_____

_____

_____

Date Completed:_____

Location:_____

Adventure Highlights and Favorite Memories:_____

_____

_____

_____

_____

_____

_____

Lessons Learned:_____

_____

_____

_____

_____

Bucket List Goal:

#55 _____

Inspiration for this Goal? _____

_____

_____

Steps to make this happen?_____

_____

_____

Date Completed:_____

Location:_____

Adventure Highlights and Favorite Memories:_____

_____

_____

_____

_____

_____

_____

Lessons Learned:_____

_____

_____

_____

_____

Bucket List Goal:

#56 _____

Inspiration for this Goal? _____

_____

_____

Steps to make this happen?_____

_____

_____

Date Completed:_____

Location:_____

Adventure Highlights and Favorite Memories:_____

_____

_____

_____

_____

_____

_____

Lessons Learned:_____

_____

_____

_____

_____

Bucket List Goal:
#57 _____

Inspiration for this Goal? _____

_____

_____

Steps to make this happen?_____

_____

_____

Date Completed:_____

Location:_____

Adventure Highlights and Favorite Memories:_____

_____

_____

_____

_____

_____

_____

Lessons Learned:_____

_____

_____

_____

_____

Bucket List Goal:
#58 _____

Inspiration for this Goal? _____

_____

_____

Steps to make this happen?_____

_____

_____

Date Completed:_____

Location:_____

Adventure Highlights and Favorite Memories:_____

_____

_____

_____

_____

_____

_____

Lessons Learned:_____

_____

_____

_____

_____

Bucket List Goal:
#59 _____

Inspiration for this Goal? _____

_____

_____

Steps to make this happen?_____

_____

_____

Date Completed:_____

Location:_____

Adventure Highlights and Favorite Memories:_____

_____

_____

_____

_____

_____

_____

Lessons Learned:_____

_____

_____

_____

_____

Bucket List Goal:
#60 _____

Inspiration for this Goal? _____
_____
_____

Steps to make this happen?_____
_____
_____

Date Completed:_____

Location:_____

Adventure Highlights and Favorite Memories:_____
_____
_____
_____
_____
_____
_____

Lessons Learned:_____
_____
_____
_____

Bucket List Goal:

#61 _____

Inspiration for this Goal? _____

_____

_____

Steps to make this happen?_____

_____

_____

Date Completed:_____

Location:_____

Adventure Highlights and Favorite Memories:_____

_____

_____

_____

_____

_____

_____

Lessons Learned:_____

_____

_____

_____

_____

Bucket List Goal:

#62 _____

Inspiration for this Goal? _____

_____

_____

Steps to make this happen?_____

_____

_____

Date Completed:_____

Location:_____

Adventure Highlights and Favorite Memories:_____

_____

_____

_____

_____

_____

_____

Lessons Learned:_____

_____

_____

_____

_____

Bucket List Goal:
#63 _____

Inspiration for this Goal? _____

_____

_____

Steps to make this happen?_____

_____

_____

Date Completed:_____

Location:_____

Adventure Highlights and Favorite Memories:_____

_____

_____

_____

_____

_____

_____

Lessons Learned:_____

_____

_____

_____

Bucket List Goal:
#64 _____

Inspiration for this Goal? _____

_____

_____

Steps to make this happen?_____

_____

_____

Date Completed:_____

Location:_____

Adventure Highlights and Favorite Memories:_____

_____

_____

_____

_____

_____

_____

Lessons Learned:_____

_____

_____

_____

Bucket List Goal:

#65 _____

Inspiration for this Goal? _____

_____

_____

Steps to make this happen?_____

_____

_____

Date Completed:_____

Location:_____

Adventure Highlights and Favorite Memories:_____

_____

_____

_____

_____

_____

_____

Lessons Learned:_____

_____

_____

_____

_____

Bucket List Goal:

#66 _____

Inspiration for this Goal? _____

_____

_____

Steps to make this happen?_____

_____

_____

Date Completed:_____

Location:_____

Adventure Highlights and Favorite Memories:_____

_____

_____

_____

_____

_____

_____

Lessons Learned:_____

_____

_____

_____

Bucket List Goal:

#67 _____

Inspiration for this Goal? _____

_____

_____

Steps to make this happen?_____

_____

_____

Date Completed:_____

Location:_____

Adventure Highlights and Favorite Memories:_____

_____

_____

_____

_____

_____

_____

Lessons Learned:_____

_____

_____

_____

Bucket List Goal:

#68 _____

Inspiration for this Goal? _____

_____

_____

Steps to make this happen?_____

_____

_____

Date Completed:_____

Location:_____

Adventure Highlights and Favorite Memories:_____

_____

_____

_____

_____

_____

_____

Lessons Learned:_____

_____

_____

_____

_____

Bucket List Goal:
#69 _____

Inspiration for this Goal? _____

_____

_____

Steps to make this happen?_____

_____

_____

Date Completed:_____

Location:_____

Adventure Highlights and Favorite Memories:_____

_____

_____

_____

_____

_____

_____

Lessons Learned:_____

_____

_____

_____

_____

Bucket List Goal:

#70 _____

Inspiration for this Goal? _____

_____

_____

Steps to make this happen?_____

_____

_____

Date Completed:_____

Location:_____

Adventure Highlights and Favorite Memories:_____

_____

_____

_____

_____

_____

_____

Lessons Learned:_____

_____

_____

_____

Bucket List Goal:
#71 _____

Inspiration for this Goal? _____

_____

_____

Steps to make this happen?_____

_____

_____

Date Completed:_____

Location:_____

Adventure Highlights and Favorite Memories:_____

_____

_____

_____

_____

_____

_____

Lessons Learned:_____

_____

_____

_____

_____

Bucket List Goal:
#72 _____

Inspiration for this Goal? _____

_____

_____

Steps to make this happen?_____

_____

_____

Date Completed:_____

Location:_____

Adventure Highlights and Favorite Memories:_____

_____

_____

_____

_____

_____

_____

Lessons Learned:_____

_____

_____

_____

_____

Bucket List Goal:

#73 _____

Inspiration for this Goal? _____

_____

_____

Steps to make this happen?_____

_____

_____

Date Completed:_____

Location:_____

Adventure Highlights and Favorite Memories:_____

_____

_____

_____

_____

_____

_____

Lessons Learned:_____

_____

_____

_____

_____

Bucket List Goal:

#74 _____

Inspiration for this Goal? _____

_____

_____

Steps to make this happen?_____

_____

_____

Date Completed:_____

Location:_____

Adventure Highlights and Favorite Memories:_____

_____

_____

_____

_____

_____

_____

Lessons Learned:_____

_____

_____

_____

_____

Bucket List Goal:

#75 _____

Inspiration for this Goal? _____

_____

_____

Steps to make this happen?_____

_____

_____

Date Completed:_____

Location:_____

Adventure Highlights and Favorite Memories:_____

_____

_____

_____

_____

_____

_____

Lessons Learned:_____

_____

_____

_____

_____

Bucket List Goal:

#76 _____

Inspiration for this Goal? _____

_____

_____

Steps to make this happen?_____

_____

_____

Date Completed:_____

Location:_____

Adventure Highlights and Favorite Memories:_____

_____

_____

_____

_____

_____

_____

Lessons Learned:_____

_____

_____

_____

_____

Bucket List Goal:

#77 _____

Inspiration for this Goal? _____

_____

_____

Steps to make this happen?_____

_____

_____

Date Completed:_____

Location:_____

Adventure Highlights and Favorite Memories:_____

_____

_____

_____

_____

_____

_____

Lessons Learned:_____

_____

_____

_____

_____

Bucket List Goal:

#78 _____

Inspiration for this Goal? _____

_____

_____

Steps to make this happen?_____

_____

_____

Date Completed:_____

Location:_____

Adventure Highlights and Favorite Memories:_____

_____

_____

_____

_____

_____

_____

Lessons Learned:_____

_____

_____

_____

Bucket List Goal:

#79 _____

Inspiration for this Goal? _____

_____

_____

Steps to make this happen?_____

_____

_____

Date Completed:_____

Location:_____

Adventure Highlights and Favorite Memories:_____

_____

_____

_____

_____

_____

_____

Lessons Learned:_____

_____

_____

_____

_____

Bucket List Goal:

#80 _____

Inspiration for this Goal? _____

_____

_____

Steps to make this happen?_____

_____

_____

Date Completed:_____

Location:_____

Adventure Highlights and Favorite Memories:_____

_____

_____

_____

_____

_____

_____

Lessons Learned:_____

_____

_____

_____

_____

Bucket List Goal:

#81 _____

Inspiration for this Goal? _____

_____

_____

Steps to make this happen?_____

_____

_____

Date Completed:_____

Location:_____

Adventure Highlights and Favorite Memories:_____

_____

_____

_____

_____

_____

_____

Lessons Learned:_____

_____

_____

_____

Bucket List Goal:
#82 _____

Inspiration for this Goal? _____
_____
_____

Steps to make this happen?_____
_____
_____

Date Completed:_____

Location:_____

Adventure Highlights and Favorite Memories:_____
_____
_____
_____
_____
_____
_____
_____

Lessons Learned:_____
_____
_____
_____
_____

Bucket List Goal:

#83 _____

Inspiration for this Goal? _____

_____

_____

Steps to make this happen?_____

_____

_____

Date Completed:_____

Location:_____

Adventure Highlights and Favorite Memories:_____

_____

_____

_____

_____

_____

_____

Lessons Learned:_____

_____

_____

_____

_____

Bucket List Goal:

#84 _____

Inspiration for this Goal? _____

_____

_____

Steps to make this happen?_____

_____

_____

Date Completed:_____

Location:_____

Adventure Highlights and Favorite Memories:_____

_____

_____

_____

_____

_____

_____

Lessons Learned:_____

_____

_____

_____

Bucket List Goal:

#85 _____

Inspiration for this Goal? _____

_____

_____

Steps to make this happen?_____

_____

_____

Date Completed:_____

Location:_____

Adventure Highlights and Favorite Memories:_____

_____

_____

_____

_____

_____

_____

Lessons Learned:_____

_____

_____

_____

Bucket List Goal:

#86 _____

Inspiration for this Goal? _____

_____

_____

Steps to make this happen?_____

_____

_____

Date Completed:_____

Location:_____

Adventure Highlights and Favorite Memories:_____

_____

_____

_____

_____

_____

_____

Lessons Learned:_____

_____

_____

_____

Bucket List Goal:

#87 _____

Inspiration for this Goal? _____

_____

_____

Steps to make this happen?_____

_____

_____

Date Completed:_____

Location:_____

Adventure Highlights and Favorite Memories:_____

_____

_____

_____

_____

_____

_____

Lessons Learned:_____

_____

_____

_____

Bucket List Goal:

#88 _____

Inspiration for this Goal? _____

_____

_____

Steps to make this happen?_____

_____

_____

Date Completed:_____

Location:_____

Adventure Highlights and Favorite Memories:_____

_____

_____

_____

_____

_____

_____

Lessons Learned:_____

_____

_____

_____

_____

Bucket List Goal:

#89 _____

Inspiration for this Goal? _____

_____

_____

Steps to make this happen?_____

_____

_____

Date Completed:_____

Location:_____

Adventure Highlights and Favorite Memories:_____

_____

_____

_____

_____

_____

_____

Lessons Learned:_____

_____

_____

_____

_____

Bucket List Goal:

#90 _____

Inspiration for this Goal? _____

_____

_____

Steps to make this happen?_____

_____

_____

Date Completed:_____

Location:_____

Adventure Highlights and Favorite Memories:_____

_____

_____

_____

_____

_____

_____

Lessons Learned:_____

_____

_____

_____

_____

Bucket List Goal:

#91 _____

Inspiration for this Goal? _____

_____

_____

Steps to make this happen?_____

_____

_____

Date Completed:_____

Location:_____

Adventure Highlights and Favorite Memories:_____

_____

_____

_____

_____

_____

_____

Lessons Learned:_____

_____

_____

_____

_____

Bucket List Goal:
#92 _____

Inspiration for this Goal? _____

_____

_____

Steps to make this happen?_____

_____

_____

Date Completed:_____

Location:_____

Adventure Highlights and Favorite Memories:_____

_____

_____

_____

_____

_____

_____

Lessons Learned:_____

_____

_____

_____

_____

Bucket List Goal:

#93 _____

Inspiration for this Goal? _____

_____

_____

Steps to make this happen?_____

_____

_____

Date Completed:_____

Location:_____

Adventure Highlights and Favorite Memories:_____

_____

_____

_____

_____

_____

_____

Lessons Learned:_____

_____

_____

_____

_____

Bucket List Goal:
#94 _____

Inspiration for this Goal? _____

_____

_____

Steps to make this happen?_____

_____

_____

Date Completed:_____

Location:_____

Adventure Highlights and Favorite Memories:_____

_____

_____

_____

_____

_____

_____

Lessons Learned:_____

_____

_____

_____

Bucket List Goal:
#95 _____

Inspiration for this Goal? _____

_____

_____

Steps to make this happen?_____

_____

_____

Date Completed:_____

Location:_____

Adventure Highlights and Favorite Memories:_____

_____

_____

_____

_____

_____

_____

Lessons Learned:_____

_____

_____

_____

Bucket List Goal:
#96 _____

Inspiration for this Goal? _____

_____

_____

Steps to make this happen?_____

_____

_____

Date Completed:_____

Location:_____

Adventure Highlights and Favorite Memories:_____

_____

_____

_____

_____

_____

_____

Lessons Learned:_____

_____

_____

_____

_____

Bucket List Goal:

#97 _____

Inspiration for this Goal? _____

_____

_____

Steps to make this happen?_____

_____

_____

Date Completed:_____

Location:_____

Adventure Highlights and Favorite Memories:_____

_____

_____

_____

_____

_____

_____

Lessons Learned:_____

_____

_____

_____

_____

Bucket List Goal:

#98 _____

Inspiration for this Goal? _____

_____

_____

Steps to make this happen?_____

_____

_____

Date Completed:_____

Location:_____

Adventure Highlights and Favorite Memories:_____

_____

_____

_____

_____

_____

_____

Lessons Learned:_____

_____

_____

_____

Bucket List Goal:

#99 _____

Inspiration for this Goal? _____

_____

_____

Steps to make this happen?_____

_____

_____

Date Completed:_____

Location:_____

Adventure Highlights and Favorite Memories:_____

_____

_____

_____

_____

_____

_____

Lessons Learned:_____

_____

_____

_____

_____

Bucket List Goal:
#100 _____

Inspiration for this Goal? _____

_____

_____

Steps to make this happen?_____

_____

_____

Date Completed:_____

Location:_____

Adventure Highlights and Favorite Memories:_____

_____

_____

_____

_____

_____

_____

Lessons Learned:_____

_____

_____

_____

Notes:

Notes:

Notes:

Notes:

Notes:

Notes:

Notes:

Notes:

Notes:

Made in the USA
Las Vegas, NV
11 December 2020